TRANSPORTATION

Ian Graham

QEB

QEB Publishing

060809

JNF
629
Gra

Copyright © QEB Publishing, Inc. 2008

Published in the United States by
QEB Publishing, Inc.
23062 La Cadena Drive
Laguna Hills, CA 92653

www.qeb-publishing.com

Library of Congress Control Number: 2008012584

ISBN 978 1 59566 603 1

Printed and bound in the United States

Author Ian Graham
Consultant Sue Becklake
Editor Amanda Askew
Designer Gaspard de Beauvais
Picture Researcher Maria Joannou
Illustrator Richard Burgess

Publisher Steve Evans
Creative Director Zeta Davies

Picture credits (t=top, b=bottom, l=left, r=right)
Alamy Images John Henshall 24–25, Guichaoua 13b
Corbis 12t, Jean Becker/Sygma 3t, 22b, Bettmann 6t, 24b, 28l,
Car Culture 8b, 8–9, Hulton-Deutsch Collection 10t,
Michael Macor/San Francisco Chronicle 7t, Carl & Ann Purcell 17t,
Reuters 16b, Eberhard Streichan/Zefa 14–15, Tim de Waele 10–11
Department of Defence 18b
DK Images 4t
Getty Images AFP Photo/Jamal Nasrallah-Files 6–7, AFP Photo/
Yoshikazu Tsuno 11t, Koichi Kamoshida 15t, Time Life Pictures/
Mansell 23t
Hawkes Ocean Technologies 21b
Istockphoto 11b
NASA 26t, 26–27, 28–29, 29b
Scaled Composites 26b
Science Photo Library Mike Agliolo 20-21
Shutterstock 3, 4–5, 5t, 12–13, 13t, 22–23, 25t
US Navy 16-17, 18-19, 19t, 21t
Virgin Trains 12b

Words in **bold** can be found in
the glossary on page 30.

Contents

INVENTIONS IN TRANSPORTATION

Hundreds of inventions have made transportation faster, easier, and safer. Some of these inventions were made by scientists and engineers working for big companies, but many of them were made by ordinary people with a bright idea.

On land

The wheel is probably the most important transportation invention ever. With the wheel, it was possible to build horse-drawn carts and carriages. Later, the invention of **engines** led to the first vehicles that could move by themselves without having to be pulled by animals.

The wheel was probably invented in Mesopotamia about 5,500 years ago to use with carts and chariots.

The largest ships today are as big as a skyscraper lying on its side.

In and on the water

For thousands of years, sea voyages relied on oar power or wind and sails—until the steam engine was invented. **Steamships** could sail even if there was no wind. Since then, inventors have found lots of new ways to travel in water.

In the air

The invention of the airplane and then the jet airliner allowed people to travel further and faster than ever before. The **jet engine** was invented by Englishman Frank Whittle and German Hans von Ohain in the 1930s. It once took about four months to travel to the other side of the world by sailing ship. Now flying there takes less than 24 hours. A few lucky people can even soar away into space and circle the whole world every 90 minutes.

INVENTIONS IN TRANSPORTATION

3500 BCE	Wheel
1620s AD	Submarine
1769	Steam-powered vehicle
1804	Steam locomotive
1852	Airship
1885	Car
1885	Motorcycle
1903	Airplane
1907	Helicopter
1949	Jet airliner
1955	Hovercraft
1961	Manned spacecraft
1964	High-speed electric train
1973	Jet Ski
1981	Space shuttle

Two billion people fly in an airliner every year. All but the smallest airliners are powered by jet engines.

KING OF THE ROAD

The invention of the car changed our everyday lives. Today, there are about 750 million cars on the roads.

Benz's 1885 car had a top speed of less than 10 miles an hour.

Steam power

In 1769, Frenchman Nicolas-Joseph Cugnot put a small **steam engine** on a cart and made the first vehicle that could move using its own **power**. It could only go at walking speed, but it showed that a cart could move on its own. Other inventors then began to make better and faster vehicles.

The first car

The car was invented in 1885 by German engineer Karl Benz. It had three wheels and was powered by a small **gasoline** engine at the back.

DID YOU KNOW?

Inventors are still coming up with new ideas for cars. Some cars can take off and fly like planes. The first flying car was the Autoplane, designed by American Glenn Curtiss in 1917, but it never took off. The first car to fly was the Aerobile, built by U.S. inventor Waldo Waterman in 1937.

The flying Moller Skycar will be able to reach a top speed of 370 miles an hour!

Supersonic *speed*

Jet cars are powered by jet engines. They were invented in the 1960s to set speed records. A car called Thrust SSC is the fastest jet car in the world. In 1997, it went 763 miles an hour—faster than the speed of sound! It could have driven across the United States from New York to Los Angeles, a distance of 2,800 miles, in about 3.5 hours. It would take about two days at normal road speeds.

Two jet engines make Thrust SSC as powerful as 145 racing cars!

INTO THE FUTURE

Nearly all cars today have engines that burn gasoline fuel. Car makers are trying out new types of car engine and new fuels for the future.

After oil

Engines that burn gasoline give out harmful gases, so some car makers are testing cleaner engines. New engines and fuels will be needed anyway because the oil that gasoline is made from will run out one day.

The Nissan Pivo is a future car powered by **electric motors** inside its wheels.

Electric cars

Cars can be powered by electric motors. The electric carriage was invented in the 1830s, but cars with gasoline engines became more popular. Now, people are interested in electric cars again because they do not burn fuel and so do not give out any harmful gases.

Hydrogen *power*

The hydrogen-powered car was invented in the 1860s, but became more widely developed in the 1970s. It uses hydrogen gas instead of gasoline. When hydrogen burns, it produces water instead of fumes. The Ford Fusion Hydrogen 999 is a car powered by hydrogen fuel cells. It can reach a speed of 205 miles an hour.

DID YOU KNOW?

In the 1890s, the fastest cars in the world were electric. In 1899, they reached a speed of 65 miles an hour and people were amazed. They thought a driver would die if he went that fast!

The BMW H2R is a hydrogen-powered racing car that can reach a top speed of 190 miles an hour.

ON TWO WHEELS

Bikes have been around for about 200 years. They have changed a lot in that time and new two-wheelers are still being developed today.

A solid back wheel and a lightweight frame lets a racing bike slip through the air faster than an ordinary bike.

Pushing pedals

Scotsman Kirkpatrick Macmillan made the first bike with pedals in 1842, but the pedals went forward and backward! The modern bicycle was invented by English inventor John Kemp Starley in 1885. His invention was the Rover safety bicycle. It had a diamond-shaped frame, equal-sized wheels, and a chain turning the back wheel.

High-wheeler or penny-farthing bikes were popular in the 1870s. The rider sat on top of the front wheel.

DID YOU KNOW?

Tires filled with air, called pneumatic tires, were invented by Scotsman Robert Thomson in 1845, but they were impractical. Then in 1888, Scotsman John Boyd Dunlop made better pneumatic tires. Dunlop's tires were a great success.

Motorcycles

The first motorcycle was built in 1885 by two German engineers, Gottlieb Daimler and Wilhelm Maybach. On November 10, 1885, Daimler's son rode it and became the world's first motorcyclist.

The future Yamaha Gen-Ryu motorbike has a gasoline engine and an electric motor.

Lean and go

One of the most advanced two-wheelers is the Segway. It was invented by American Dean Kamen in 2001. The rider stands on a platform and holds onto the handle. Electric motors turn the wheels. Whichever way you lean, that is the way it goes.

The Segway is easy to ride because it balances by itself.

ON THE TRACKS

Trains were invented in the early 1800s. They were steam powered. Today, high-speed electric trains whisk passengers from city to city as fast as racing cars. Japan's bullet train was the first high-speed train.

The first railway line across the United States was built in 1869.

Steam power

The steam **locomotive**, the engine that pulls a train, was invented by Richard Trevithick in Britain in 1804. The first locomotives were used in mines and ironworks to move heavy wagons of coal and iron.

Tilting passenger trains, such as the Pendolino, are used in several European countries.

Tilting trains

Passenger trains can go round bends faster if they tilt. Tilting stops things sliding off the tables. The first tilting trains were built in Spain in the 1950s.

Japan's 500 series bullet train is one of the fastest passenger trains in the world. It has a top speed of 190 miles an hour.

Bullet trains

The first high-speed train, named the bullet train, was invented in Japan in 1964. New railroads were built specially for the trains so that they could go as fast as possible. Since they started running, they have carried about six billion passengers.

DID YOU KNOW?
The TGV set a passenger train speed record of 356 miles an hour in 2007—nearly twice as fast as a racing car.

TGV

France's high-speed train service is called Train à Grande Vitesse or TGV, meaning high-speed train. It started running in 1981. It worked so well that similar high-speed trains were built in other countries, such as the United States, Spain, and South Korea.

High-speed trains, such as the TGV, are sleek and **streamlined** so that they can slip through the air as fast as possible.

FLYING TRAINS

The most advanced trains float above the track. Magnets **lift the trains into the air and fly them along the railroad.**

Magnetic marvels

Flying trains are called **maglevs**. People started thinking about using magnets to make a train float in the air in the early 1900s. Work started on the first maglevs in the 1960s, mainly in Japan and Germany.

Maglevs in Germany are tested on this special track.

Transrapid

Europa

DID YOU KNOW?

The first high-speed maglev railroad opened in China in 2002. It carries passengers between the city of Shanghai and its airport.

Low-flying trains

The first maglev was opened to the public in Birmingham, England. From 1984 to 1995, it carried passengers between the city's airport and railroad station. The trains were **automatic**—there were no drivers. They traveled at a speed of 26 miles an hour.

In 2003, a Japanese maglev set the world record speed of 361 miles an hour.

Super fliers

The fastest maglevs can travel at a greater speed than other trains because they do not touch the track. They cannot go on ordinary railroads. Special tracks called guideways are built.

Magnets in the train and track raise the train above the track.

Track

Train

Train magnet

Track magnet

ON THE WATER

Boats can go faster if they fly above the surface of the water instead of traveling through it.

> The invention of the sailing ship led to great voyages of discovery.

First boats

Boats have been used as transportation for thousands of years. The ancient Egyptians traveled along the Nile River by boat, and many people built ships for war.

When a hydrofoil rises up out of the water, it is not bumped about by the waves and so it gives passengers a smoother ride.

Hydrofoil

One way to make a boat travel above water is to use wings. They work like a plane's wings, but underwater. When the hydrofoil speeds up, the underwater wings lift it out of the water. When it slows down, the boat sits in the water again.

Hovercraft

In the 1950s, English engineer and inventor Christopher Cockerell built a new type of vehicle—a hovercraft. Air is blown down underneath a hovercraft, pushing it up above the water. A hovercraft can skim over land just as easily as water—so it can go places that a boat cannot.

The U.S. Navy uses hovercraft to bring soldiers and equipment ashore from ships.

DID YOU KNOW?

In 1965, American Clayton Jacobson II invented the Sea-Doo. It scooted across the water like a floating motorcycle. It was not a success. When the Jet Ski was introduced in 1973, it was a big hit.

FULL STEAM AHEAD

Steam power seems old-fashioned today, but the most advanced warships and submarines **still rely on steam. Their engines are nuclear-powered steam engines.**

Nuclear fuel

Most ships have engines that burn a fuel such as gasoline or oil. A nuclear-powered ship or submarine is different. Its **nuclear fuel**, uranium, gets very hot on its own and it stays hot for years. The heat boils water, which changes into steam. The steam drives generators that make electricity and also turns the **propellers**.

The US Navy's *Nautilus* was the first nuclear-powered submarine. It was launched in 1954.

Nuclear vessels

The first nuclear-powered vessels were built in the 1950s. With nuclear power, a submarine can stay hidden underwater for several months. Nuclear-powered warships can go anywhere in the world's oceans without having to keep stopping for fuel.

Catapults on ships

Ships called **aircraft carriers** use steam in another way. Planes take off from an aircraft carrier's deck. A plane has to be going fast enough to take off when it gets to the end of the deck or it will fall into the sea. To give it some extra speed, a huge catapult powered by steam hurls the plane along the deck. The idea to use steam in this way came from Commander Colin Mitchell of the British Royal Navy in 1950.

A steam catapult sends a fighter flying off the deck of an aircraft carrier.

The US Navy's giant *Nimitz* aircraft carrier has four propellers driven by steam from two **nuclear reactors**.

DID YOU KNOW?

A *Nimitz* warship has eight steam-powered generators producing enough electricity for a small city.

GOING UNDER

Inventors started trying to build submarines 400 years ago. Today, giant submarines cruise the oceans and tiny diving craft called submersibles **explore the seabed.**

First submarines

The first person to design a submarine was Englishman William Bourne in 1578, but he did not build it. Dutchman Cornelis Drebbel built the first submarine in the 1620s. It was a wooden boat covered with greased leather to stop water getting in. Twelve oarsmen rowed it underwater in the River Thames in London, England.

Modern subs

The modern submarine was developed by the American John P. Holland. A submarine was bought by the US Navy. Others soon bought their own. Submarines were widely used in World War I (1914–1918) and World War II. The German

Submarines dive by letting seawater flood into tanks to make them heavier.

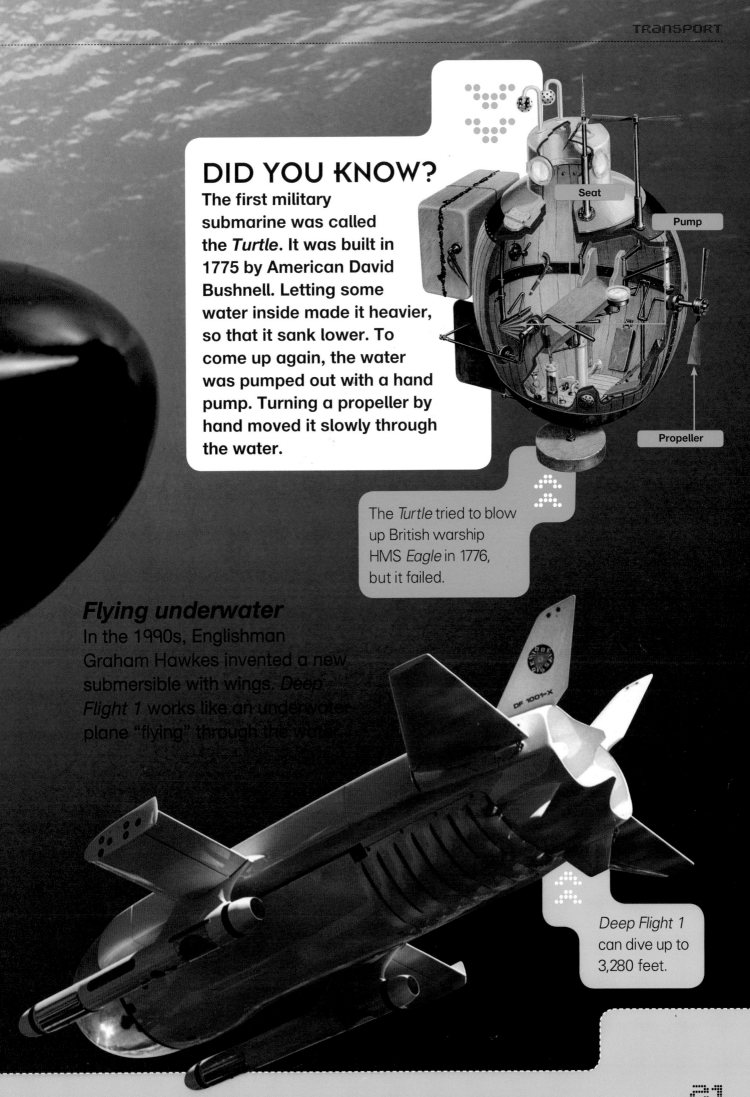

DID YOU KNOW?

The first military submarine was called the *Turtle*. It was built in 1775 by American David Bushnell. Letting some water inside made it heavier, so that it sank lower. To come up again, the water was pumped out with a hand pump. Turning a propeller by hand moved it slowly through the water.

Seat

Pump

Propeller

The *Turtle* tried to blow up British warship HMS *Eagle* in 1776, but it failed.

Flying underwater

In the 1990s, Englishman Graham Hawkes invented a new submersible with wings. *Deep Flight 1* works like an underwater plane "flying" through the water.

DF 1001-X

Deep Flight 1 can dive up to 3,280 feet.

TAKE-OFF

The first flights were made by people in balloons, but balloons floated wherever the wind blew them. Inventors soon started looking for ways of making flying machines that they could steer.

Hot-air balloons

Hot air is lighter than cold air. Smoke rises from a fire because hot air floats upward and carries the smoke up with it. In 1783, two French brothers, Joseph and Étienne Montgolfier, filled a big balloon with hot air and watched it rise up over Paris with two brave passengers. It was the first manned flight.

In 1999, *Breitling Orbiter 3* made the first balloon flight around the world without landing.

The Wright brothers

Orville and Wilbur Wright were bicycle makers from Dayton, Ohio. In the early 1900s, they built **gliders** and flew them. Then in 1903, they built an aircraft with an engine. On 17 December 1903, Orville used it to make the first airplane flight at Kitty Hawk, North Carolina.

The Wright brothers' airplane, Flyer, took off for the first ever powered flight in 1903.

Modern aircraft

Aircraft today are marvels of engineering. Their designers make use of the latest inventions in materials, engines, electronics, and computers to produce the best possible aircraft. The European plane maker, Airbus, produced nearly 400 inventions of its own for the new A380 airliner.

The biggest airliner in the world is the Airbus A380. Each of its giant wings is about 130 feet in length.

DID YOU KNOW?

The first flight of the Wright Flyer only lasted for 12 seconds. It flew 118 feet at an average speed of 7 miles an hour. Longer flights soon followed.

SPINNING BLADES

Helicopters can take off straight up in the air and hover in one place. They can fly like this because they have spinning blades.

The first helicopter

The first person to take off and fly using spinning blades was Frenchman Paul Cornu in 1907. He only just managed to get off the ground for a few seconds. It was another 30 years before helicopters could stay in the air for an hour.

A year after its first short flight in 1940, Sikorsky's helicopter set a new world record by staying in the air for more than 90 minutes.

Helicopters today

The modern helicopter was developed by Russian-American Igor Sikorsky in 1940. His helicopter had a big set of blades at the top and a small set at the end of its tail. Helicopters are still built like this today.

A helicopter's ability to hover and to land vertically makes it ideal for search and rescue work and police air patrols.

The Osprey is a tiltrotor. It takes off like a helicopter, then its engines tilt down and it flies like a plane.

Tiltrotors

Tiltrotors are planes with swiveling engines. With the engines tilted up, the propellers work like helicopter blades and lift the plane straight up. The tiltrotor was invented in the USA in 1954.

DID YOU KNOW?

Igor Sikorsky was born in Kiev, Ukraine, in 1889. He built the first plane with four engines in 1913. He moved to the United States in 1919 and built passenger planes. Then he built the first successful helicopter. He died in 1972.

INTO SPACE

Until the 1960s, the idea of traveling into space was just a dream. Since then, more than 460 people from 34 countries have gone into space.

Early manned **spacecraft**, such as the U.S. Mercury capsules, were tiny—just big enough for one person to fit inside.

First into space

The first manned spacecraft, *Vostok 1*, was launched in 1961. Russian pilot Yuri Gagarin sat inside the tiny ball-shaped craft. He flew around the world once and landed. The whole flight took 108 minutes.

Spaceplanes

Early manned spacecraft could only be used once. Then in 1981, the space agency, NASA, launched a new type of manned spacecraft called the **space shuttle**. It can be used many times.

SpaceShipOne won a prize of $10 million by flying into space in 2004. It was the first manned spacecraft launched by a private company, not a space agency, such as NASA.

Soyuz spacecraft

Russia's manned spacecraft is called Soyuz. It made its first manned flight in 1967. Today, the latest type of Soyuz spacecraft carries **astronauts** to the **International Space Station** and brings them back to Earth again.

A Soyuz spacecraft carries a **crew** of three astronauts.

DID YOU KNOW?

Vostok 1 launched the first man into space. *Vostok 2* was the first manned spacecraft to spend more than one day in space. *Vostok 6* launched the first woman into space.

ROCKETS AND SHUTTLES

Spaceflight depends on rockets **because they are the only vehicles powerful enough to launch spacecraft.**

Robert Goddard's rocket only rose to a height of 39 feet, but it showed that liquid-fuel rockets could work.

Rockets

Spacecraft, such as the U.S. space shuttle and Russian Soyuz, are launched by rockets. Rockets that burn solid fuel were invented in China about 1,000 years ago. Most big space rockets burn liquid fuel. This type of rocket was invented by U.S. scientist Robert Goddard in 1926. He launched a small rocket from his aunt's farm in Auburn, Massachusetts.

Two giant, solid-fuel rocket boosters supply most of the power needed to lift the space shuttle off its launch pad.

Space shuttle

The space shuttle has three parts—the Orbiter, the external tank, and the solid-fuel rocket boosters. The Orbiter is the spaceplane the crew travels in. The external tank holds fuel for three rocket engines in the Orbiter's tail. The boosters add more power. The tank and boosters fall back to Earth, while the Orbiter flies on into space.

DID YOU KNOW?

At the end of a mission, the space shuttle Orbiter re-enters the Earth's atmosphere at 25 times the speed of sound.

The space shuttle usually carries a crew of up to seven astronauts.

GLOSSARY

Aircraft carrier
A large warship used by the navy, so aircraft can take off and land at sea.

Astronaut
A person who travels in space.

Automatic
Works without human control.

Crew
The person or people who work in a ship, submarine, aircraft, or spacecraft.

Electric motor
A machine that changes electricity into movement.

Engine
A machine that uses power to make a vehicle, such as a car, move.

Fuel
Something that is burned in an engine to produce power.

Gasoline
A fuel made from oil for burning inside an engine.

Glider
An aircraft with wings but no engine.

Hydrogen
The lightest gas of all.

International Space Station
A giant manned spacecraft being built in space near the Earth.

Jet engine
A machine that burns fuel to make a jet of gas that can move a plane through the air.

Locomotive
A railroad engine that pulls a train.

Maglev
A train that is lifted into the air by magnets so that it flies along just above its track. Maglev is short for magnetic levitation.

Magnet
A piece of iron or other material that can attract or repel similar objects.

Nuclear fuel
Something that gives out energy due to nuclear reactions.

Nuclear reactor
A device or structure containing nuclear fuel and giving out nuclear energy.

Pneumatic
Containing a gas, such as air, that is under pressure.

Power
The amount of work done every second.

Propeller
A set of spinning blades that moves an aircraft through the air.

Rocket
A vehicle that flies through space using a jet of gas produced by burning fuel.

Spacecraft
Manned or unmanned vehicles that fly in space.

Spaceplane
A spacecraft with wings for taking astronauts into space and bringing them back to Earth.

Space shuttle
A U.S. spaceplane launched by rockets that is able to land on a runway like an airplane.

Steam engine
A machine that heats water to make steam and uses the steam to do work.

Steamship
A ship powered by a steam engine.

Streamlined
Having a smooth, gently curving shape that moves through the air easily.

Submarine
A sealed boat that can dive underwater and come back up to the surface again.

Submersible
A small diving craft that is used to explore the seabed.

Supersonic
Faster than the speed of sound.

Index